Will it si...

Written by Clare Helen Welsh
Photographed by Will Amlot

Collins

Zac has a shell.

Will it sink?

Yes, the shell sinks.

Will this sink?

Yes, the fox sinks.

Will this sink?

Yes, the van sinks.

Will this sink?

No.

The cup will not sink.

The cup fills ...

and then sinks!

/w/

14

/y/

 Review: After reading

Use your assessment from hearing the children read to choose any GPCs, words or tricky words that need additional practice.

Read 1: Decoding

- Look through the book with the children and ask them to find a word with the /x/ sound in it. (*fox*)
- Can the children think of any words that rhyme with **sink**? (e.g. *pink, think, wink, link, clink, blink*) These words all end in the /nk/ sound.
- Look at the "I spy sounds" pages (14–15). Discuss the picture with the children. Can they find items/ examples of words with the /w/ sound or the /y/ sound? (*water bottle, whale, wheels, wool, watch, whistle, yellow, yo-yo, yarn*)

Read 2: Prosody

- Model reading each page with expression to the children. After you have read each page, ask the children to have a go at reading with expression.
- On page 3, 5, 7 and 9 show the children how you use a questioning voice for the questions.

Read 3: Comprehension

- For every question ask the children how they know the answer. Ask:
  - What are the children testing? (*whether items sink or float*)
  - Which items in the book sink? (*van, fox, shell, the cup when it fills with water*)
  - Which items in the book float? (*the empty cup*)
  - Look at pages 4 and 5. What does the tick mean? (*yes, it will sink*) What does the cross mean? (*no, it will not sink*)
  - What items would you like to test?
  - What would you need to carry out a sinking and floating investigation? (*water, a container, items/ objects to test*)